ROBIN HOOD

The Taxman

STARTER LEVEL

Adapted by: Fiona Beddall

Publisher: Jacquie Bloese

Editor: Cheryl Pelteret

Designer: Mo Choy

Picture research: Emma Bree

Photo credits:

Cover and interior images © Tiger Aspect Productions 2006
Pages 28 & 29: The Art Archive, The Barnes Foundation/
Corbis; Mary Evans/Alamy

Based on the original story by Richard Kurti & Bev Doyle.
Based on the television series created by Foz Allan and
Dominic Minghella.

BBC & logo © and ™ BBC 1996

Robin Hood logo ™ and © Tiger Aspect Productions 2006.
Licensed by BBC Worldwide Ltd.

All rights reserved.

Published by Scholastic Ltd. 2008

Mary Glasgow Magazines (Scholastic Ltd.)
Euston House
24 Eversholt Street
London NW1 1DB

Printed in Malaysia.

Reprinted in 2009, 2012 and 2014.

Contents

ROBIN HOOD

ROBIN

MUCH

LITTLE JOHN

WILL

ALLAN

DJAQ

ROBIN HOOD is from a rich family with a big house. But now Sir Guy of Gisborne lives in Robin's house and Robin lives in Sherwood Forest. Robin takes money from rich people and gives it to poor people.

LITTLE JOHN, MUCH, ALLAN, WILL and **DJAQ** live with Robin in Sherwood Forest, They help him in his work.

4

MARIAN is from a rich family. She and Robin are old friends. She likes helping people and hates the Sheriff and Sir Guy.

THE ABBESS OF RUFFORD arrives suddenly at Nottingham Castle after an attack in Sherwood Forest.

THE SHERIFF governs the town of Nottingham. He takes lots of taxes from poor people so they don't have money for food. He hates Robin Hood. But can he stop Robin's work?

SIR GUY works for the Sheriff. Many people are dead because of him. He hates Robin Hood but he loves Marian.

FLAXTON and **CEDRIC** Flaxton is a taxman. His son, Cedric, works with him.

EDWARD is Marian's father. He isn't happy because Marian is working with Robin Hood and his men. It is very dangerous for Marian, and for Edward too.

PLACES

Sherwood Forest
The road to Nottingham goes through this big forest. Robin lives here with his men.

Nottingham Castle
The Sheriff and his guards live here.
Knighton Hall
Marian and her father, Edward, live in this big house.

ROBIN HOOD
The Taxman

At Nottingham Castle, the Sheriff is talking to two men.

We can do it.

Don't make any mistakes or you're dead.

Here's some money now. You can have £500 when I've got Robin Hood.

A nun arrives at the castle.

Help me!

What's wrong?

An attack! Men in the forest! I ...

Guards! Take her into the castle and find a doctor.

Robin's friends are in Sherwood Forest.

Stop! We're taking your money.

We are poor. We've got some food, but no money.

That is the Sheriff's. Put it back.

And what is this?

He's a taxman!

Come here, taxman!

Please, no! He isn't a taxman!

Marian is in the garden of Knighton Hall.

Marian, Sir Guy is here.

Sir Guy! Hello.

Marian and Sir Guy go into the house.

This is for you.

That's the second thing this week, Sir Guy! I don't …

Please, Marian. I want to be your friend … maybe one day your husband.

I don't want a husband, Sir Guy.

It is dangerous for a woman without a husband, Marian. Men in Sherwood Forest are attacking women on the road to Nottingham. There is an abbess at the castle today ... I want to talk to her about the terrible attack ...

Then go to her now. You have important work, Sir Guy. Please, go.

Goodbye, then, Marian.

Sir Guy is leaving. Why is he angry, Marian?

Because I don't want a husband ... I don't want *him*.

Sir Guy is an important man, Marian – a good husband for you.

I hate Sir Guy … Maybe I can be a nun. Nuns don't have husbands.

I don't understand you, Marian. You don't want a husband. You go out every night and help Robin Hood and his men. It's dangerous. Do you want to be dead soon? Stop this, now!

I can't stop. People have no food. Without my help, their children don't eat.

Stop, or leave this house.

I can't stop, so …

Where are you going? Marian? Marian!

Sir Guy is back at Nottingham Castle. He's telling the Sheriff about the abbess.

An attack in Sherwood Forest. Robin Hood, I think. The poor woman is very tired after a night in the forest.

Well, we don't want her here. I hate nuns. Who pays for their expensive food and beautiful homes? We do! But they never say thank you to us. They only say thank you to God.

Don't worry. I'm leaving tomorrow. And I can pay you for today's food.

Good.

Now, I want to talk to God. Where is your chapel?

The chapel isn't open today. You can't go in.

The chapel is God's house, Sheriff. You can't close God's house.

Well, I can talk to the guards …

12

In Sherwood Forest.

So, what can you tell us, Flaxton? Or do you want a dead son?

The tax money from fifty towns is in Nottingham Castle.

Fifty towns?! But why?

I don't know. But the money goes to the castle every September.

That's true. My father always makes new tax chests for the Sheriff in September.

I want that money.

But you can't take the money. There are hundreds of guards at the castle.

He's right. What about the guards?

We can't do it, Robin.

That money is for people's food. I want that money before they take it to London.

Will's mother is dead because of your taxes. Lots of people are dead. They haven't got any money for food. We're giving the money back to the people.

But … how?

Where in the castle is the money?

In the strongroom. But you can't go in …

Good! So we aren't going!

We can't go into the strongroom, Much. But he can.

The Sheriff is in the chapel with his guards.

Good. The abbess can't see the tax chests now. She can come and talk to her God.

This is dangerous, Sheriff.

Hello, Abbess. Now, when you want to leave the chapel, tell the guards. They can open the doors for you.

You are locking me into the chapel?! God is watching you, Sheriff. Remember that.

God doesn't govern Nottingham, Abbess. I do. Goodbye.

Flaxton and Will go to the castle.

I'm here for the taxes.

Right, then. Come with me.

Robin and his friends are watching Flaxton. Robin sees Marian. She looks sad.

Robin!

Hello, Marian! What's wrong?

Where do I start?! Sir Guy … my father … I can't live like this, Robin. I'm leaving home.

Where are you going?

I don't know.

Robin! The castle!

Sorry, I want to help, Marian. But not now. I …

Don't worry about it. Go!

Marian goes to the chapel.

Abbess, can I talk to you for a minute?

Yes, my child.

I want to be a nun. Can I live with you at Rufford … ?

16

Robin and his friends go into the castle. Will helps them.

The strongroom is down here.

Aaaarrrggh!

Right, this is the door to the strongroom. Where's Cedric? Tell me! Where's my son?

Quiet! Not now!

Flaxton closes the door.

So this is the strongroom!

Ha! Now they can't get out!

Flaxton goes to the Sheriff.

Robin and his men are in your strongroom.

Very good! Let's go and laugh at them.

Before that, I want my £500, please.

Pay him, Sir Guy.

Will looks at the locks on the chests. They aren't his father's work. They are the same as the locks on the door! He takes the locks from the chests and ...

People are coming!

Right. Let's go!

... Will opens the door! Robin and his friends leave the strongroom.

The Sheriff sees Robin.

It's Robin Hood! Guards!

The guards attack Robin Hood and his men.

So you are leaving tonight.

I am meeting the Abbess of Rufford in one hour.

Marian, don't go. Please. What can I do?

Help me. Help me in my work with poor people. And don't leave me in the same room as Sir Guy.

It is dangerous. I can't ... .

Goodbye then, Father.

Wait, Marian. I don't want to live without you. You can have my help.

Thank you.

Djaq is waiting in Sherwood Forest with Cedric. She hears her friends.

Where's Cedric?

He's there.

Look! He's going!

Let's go! Run!

Twenty minutes later ...

Cedric!

Have you got the tax money?

Yes! It's in these chests! We're rich!

No, you aren't! Stop! We're taking those chests.

Making ROBIN HOOD

Harry Lloyd (Will) with a make-up artist

A famous Englishman in a beautiful English forest. Right?

Wrong! You aren't looking at England when you watch *Robin Hood*. They make *Robin Hood* in Budapest, Hungary. There's a big forest there, and a castle from a 1980s film.

TV work is easy. Right?

Wrong! One day of filming makes only five minutes of *Robin Hood* on TV. And the days are very long.

A DAY OF FILMING

6.00: The make-up artists start work. They work on every actor for 25 minutes. Black eyes and wounds can take many hours.

7.00: It's breakfast time. The actors eat on a bus.

7.15: The cameramen start work.

9.00: The cameras and lights are ready. Filming starts.

13.00: It's time for lunch on the bus, and lots of nice Hungarian food.

20.00: It's the end of a long day of work. The actors have a drink in Budapest, or they go to bed – *they're* starting work again before seven tomorrow morning!

Jonas Armstrong (Robin) reads the newspaper when he isn't working.

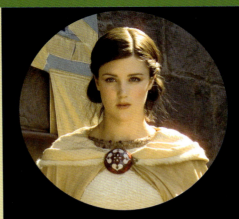

"I get up at 5.45 every day. Then I have three hours with my make-up artist before filming. I love my job, but in August it's very hot under these clothes!"

Lucy Griffiths (Marian)

"We do the fights lots of times before filming. Sometimes the fights are dangerous for the actors. I haven't got one of my teeth now!"

Keith Allen (the Sheriff)

"We're in Hungary for six months of the year. It's fun, but I don't often see my family. My children don't recognise me when I come home!"

Gordon Kennedy (Little John)

Do you want a job in TV? Why / Why not?
What job do you want?

What do these words mean? You can use a dictionary.

filming make-up artist actor wound camera(man) fight recognise

Time travel: England

Hello, time travellers! England in 1200 is a very different place from England today. Come and meet some of the children from the time of Robin Hood.

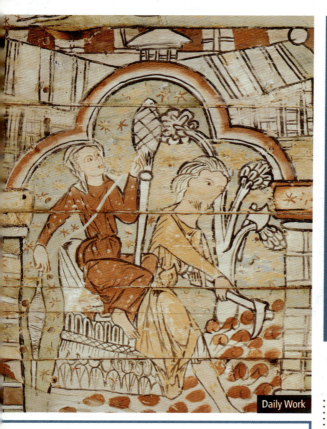

Daily Work

Marian in *Robin Hood* is 21. That's very old for a girl with no husband.

CECILY doesn't go to school – there aren't any schools in her town. She helps her mother with her work. They make cloth and work in their garden. She's twelve years old – ready for marriage. She likes a boy in her town, but he's from a very poor family. She can't be his wife. Marriage isn't about love, it's about money. Her father is looking for a good husband for her.

What is good and bad about life for teenagers in Robin Hood's England?

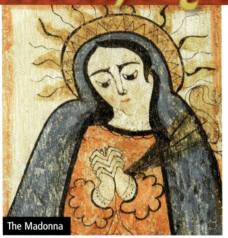
The Madonna

EDWARD is eleven and he comes from an important family. He wants to be a knight. He doesn't live with his family. He lives in a castle and has lessons there. He can read, but his important lessons are horseriding and swordfighting. There are very young boys at the castle with him. Some are only seven.

ELEANOR is fourteen years old. She lives in a convent and wants to be a nun. She sees her family every month, but she can never leave the convent. She can read and write – she has lessons from the nuns. But nuns can't dance or eat nice food, and they can't have husbands or children. Eleanor goes to the chapel at 2 o'clock every night, and five times every day. She helps in the convent hospital too.

A Knight

An abbess governs the nuns in a convent. In 1200, it is the only good job for a woman without an important husband.

Robin Hood and Sir Guy of Gisborne are knights. They are good at swordfighting after years of lessons like Edward's.

What do these words mean? You can use a dictionary.

travel(ler)   cloth   marriage   knight   convent   horseriding   swordfighting

PAGES 6–11

Before you read
You can use your dictionary for these questions.

1 This story is about Robin Hood. What do you know about him?

2 Discuss these questions.
   a) Are there any **castles** in your country? What are they like?
   b) What can you see in a **forest**?
   c) Is your town dangerous at night? Are there sometimes **attacks** in the streets?
   d) Who **governs** your country?
   e) What jobs do the very **rich** people in your country do?

3 Which two people live in the same place? What job do the other people do?
   an abbess   a taxman   a nun   a guard

4 Read 'People and Places' on pages 4 and 5. Who takes lots of money from the Sheriff in this story, do you think?

After you read
4 Write the names.
   Robin   the Sheriff   Marian   Edward   Flaxton   Sir Guy
   a) … gives money to two men at the castle.
   b) … helps the Abbess after an attack in the forest.
   c) … helps Robin at night.
   d) … doesn't understand his daughter.
   e) … is a taxman.
   f) … asks Flaxton about his book.

5 Who says this? Who to? What are they talking about?
   a) 'Don't make any mistakes or you're dead.'
   b) 'That is the Sheriff's. Put it back.'
   c) 'Then go to her now. You have important work.'
   d) 'Do you want to be dead soon?'

6 Does Marian leave home in this story, do you think?

PAGES 12–18

Before you read

7 Write the words.

chest   god   chapel   lock   strongroom

a) I don't want people in my room so I always … the door.
b) Nuns go to … every day.
c) His money is in a … . No one can go in there without a guard.
d) 'Where are the papers?' 'In the … under the window.'
e) Allah is the Arabic word for … .

8 Guess the answers to these questions. Then read and check.

a) Robin and his men go to the castle. Why?
b) Marian goes to the castle too. Why?
c) Does Flaxton help Robin?

After you read

9 Are these sentences right (✓) or wrong (✗)? Change any mistakes.

a) The Sheriff likes helping nuns.
b) There is a lot of tax money in Nottingham Castle.
c) Will's mother lives in London.
d) Will goes into the castle with Flaxton.
e) Marian is sad.
f) Robin helps Marian.
g) Robin doesn't find any money in the strongroom.

10 Match the places with the sentences a–d.

Rufford   the chapel (x2)   the strongroom   the castle

a) There are a lot of guards here.
b) The tax chests are here.
c) Robin and his men can't get out of here.
d) Marian wants to live here.
e) The Abbess wants to talk to God here.

11 What do you think?

a) Why does Will want the taxes?
b) Why does Flaxton lock the door of the strongroom?
c) Why aren't the tax chests in the strongroom?

PAGES 19–25

Before you read

12 How does the story end? Think about these people.
- **a)** Robin and his men **b)** the Abbess **c)** the Sheriff
- **d)** Marian **e)** Flaxton and Cedric

Guess, then read and check.

After you read

13 What happens first? And then what happens next? Write 1–6.
- **a)** Cedric meets Flaxton and the Abbess.
- **b)** Will unlocks the strongroom door.
- **c)** The Sheriff finds the Abbess's clothes.
- **d)** The Sheriff sees Robin and his men.
- **e)** The Sheriff gives Flaxton some money.
- **f)** Robin and his men leave the castle.

14 Choose the right words.
- **a)** Who is Flaxton working with?
  i) the Sheriff **ii)** Robin **iii)** the Abbess
- **b)** At the start of the story, who attacks the Abbess in the forest?
  i) the Sheriff's guards **ii)** Robin's men **iii)** there is no attack
- **c)** Where does Marian live at the end of the story?
  i) Nottingham Castle **ii)** Knighton Hall **iii)** Rufford
- **d)** How does Robin find the tax money?
  i) He runs after Cedric. **ii)** He goes to the chapel.
  iii) He runs after Flaxton.
- **e)** At the end of the story, who has the tax money?
  i) the poor people of Nottingham **ii)** the Sheriff
  iii) Flaxton and the Abbess

15 Talk with a friend. You are two of Robin's men and you have got the Sheriff's tax money. What do you want to do with it?

16 What do you think?
- **a)** How can Marian's father help her?
- **b)** Robin and his men hate taxes. In your country, are taxes a good thing or a bad thing?
- **c)** Who is your favourite person in this story? Why?
- **d)** What is your favourite part of this story? Why?